Safe and Simple
SCIENCE TRICKS

Written by Fran Pickering

TOPTHAT! Kids™

Tricky Business

Science is about finding out how things work.

What? How? Why?

Scientists are curious people. Performing science tricks helps them to find answers to lots of questions!

They like to find out:
- **how something works**
- **why it does what it does**
- **where it comes from**
- **what it is made of**

Scientists use their imaginations to see the magic in ordinary things.

Scientrific!

Sometimes science experiments are like magic tricks. This book will show you how to amaze your friends and family with mind-boggling science tricks.

Here at the Top That! science laboratories we have been working hard on some fun tricks you and our young scientists can perform together to find out more about SCIENCE!

HAVE FUN!

Getting Started

Before you start to do any of the science tricks you need to make sure you are prepared and safe.

Some of the science tricks that you are going to be doing can get a bit messy, so you will need to make sure you cover your work surface with some newspaper.

You will find scissors, string and sticky tape useful for some of the science tricks.

Safe Science

Sensible scientists follow safe rules. All the science tricks in this book are safe to do, but make sure you stick to the rules.

⚠ Never, ever use hot water without asking permission first.

⚠ Always ask an adult to help you when you use a knife or scissors.

⚠ Do not experiment near food or drink.

⚠ Wash your hands after an experiment.

Your Pack

Inside your kit you will find all the equipment you need to begin the cool science tricks in this book. Take a look at the fab goggles, magnets, mirror board and table-tennis ball, plus lots more!

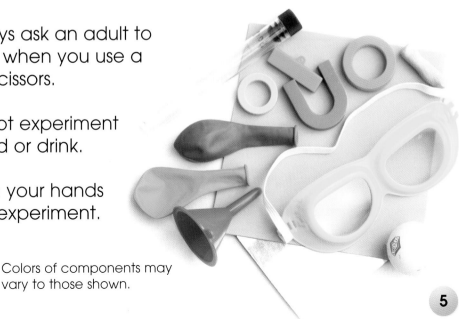

Colors of components may vary to those shown.

Let There Be Light!

Rainbows appear in the sky when sunlight shines through raindrops and splits into separate colors.

You will need:
- a torch
- a clear, shallow tray full of water
- mirror board from your kit
- white paper or cardboard

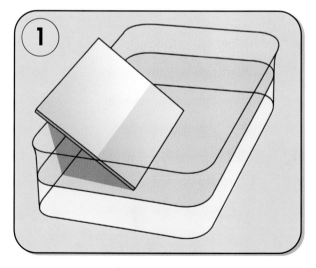

1. Fill the tray half full with water. Stand the mirror in the water so it leans against the side of the tray at an angle.

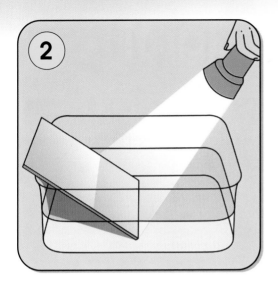

2. Turn on your torch and point it so that the light beam shines on the mirror underneath the water.

3. Hold a white piece of paper or cardboard in front and above the mirror until the reflected light shines on the paper.

What do you see?

Let There Be Light!

The paper is magically glowing with lots of rainbow colors—want to know how it works?

Rainbow Glow

Light may look white, but it is really made up of seven different colors: red, orange, yellow, green, blue, indigo and violet. These are the colors of the rainbow.

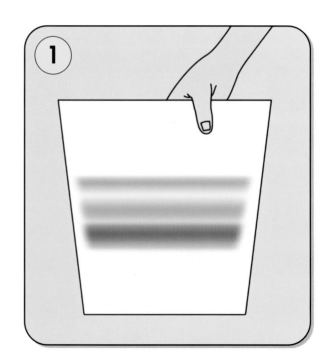

What Happens!

When the light moves through the water, it slows down and bends. The seven colors that make up the light all travel at different speeds, so when they hit the water the different colors become separated. The mirror reflects the colors so that you can see them.

Magnet Magic

1. The Levitating Paper Clip

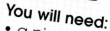

You will need:
- a piece of thread
- a paper clip
- a magnet from your kit

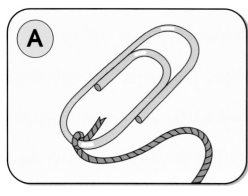

A. Tie a paper clip to a piece of thread. Hold the thread and allow the paper clip to move towards the magnet.

B. As the paper clip tries to reach the magnet, hold it back until it looks like the paper clip is levitating.

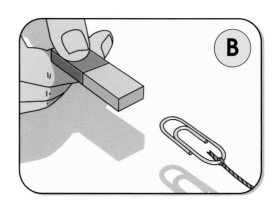

2. Magnet Maze

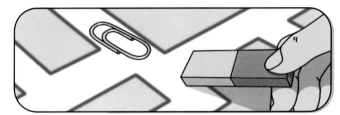

Draw a maze onto a piece of cardboard, or paper, and use the magnet to guide a paper clip through it.

3. Water Rescue

Drop a paper clip into a glass of water. See if you can rescue the paper clip, using the magnet, without getting it wet.

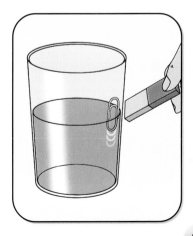

Magnet Magic

1. The paper clip is levitating.
2. The paper clip moves through the maze.
3. The paper clip rises through the water.

Opposites Attract

All magnets have two ends (or poles) that are positive and negative. If you put two of the poles together they will either pull together or push apart. Push together two of the magnets from your kit and see if you can tell if the poles are negative or positive.

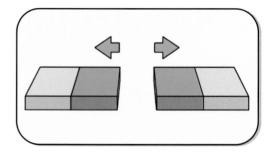

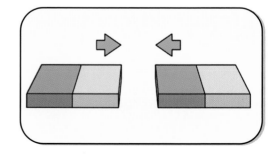

What happens!

If you hold a steel paper clip close to a magnet you can feel it being pulled towards the magnet by an invisible force called magnetism.

A force is what we say when we mean a push or a pull. These tricks show how the force of magnetism can pull paper clips. They show that magnetic forces can travel through things like glass and even water!

Science of Sound

1. Anyone There?

You will need:
- two plastic cups or clean yogurt pots
- a piece of string (2 yards long)
- scissors (ask an adult to help you with these)
- a friend

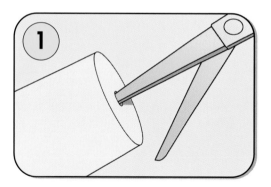

1. Carefully make a hole in the bottom of each cup.

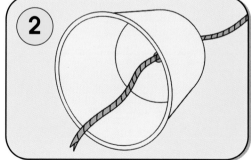

2. Poke an end of string through each cup.

3. Tie a large knot inside each cup, to stop the string slipping out.

4. Give your friend one cup. Take the other and walk as far away as you can, until the string is straight and tight.

5. One person talks into their cup while the other listens.

What happens?

Science Of Sound

You can hear each other's voices in the plastic cups.

What happens!

The sound of your voice travels along the string, which vibrates as the sound waves are pushed against it.

Hello
How are you?
I am fine.

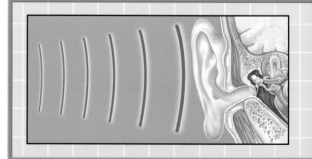

Good Vibrations

Music is really just sound vibrations controlled by the instrument and its player. When a guitarist plucks or strums the strings on a guitar, it creates vibrations. These vibrations make sounds.

Where are you?

I am at home.

Sound travels in waves through the air. You can't see them, but when the waves reach your ears, your eardrums vibrate and tell your brain that you have heard a noise.

17

Glorious Gravity

If you hold an object in the air and let go, it will fall to the ground. Which will fall faster—a large or a small object? A heavy or a light object? Find out.

1. Drop It

You will need:
- a cotton spool
- a ball or the table-tennis ball in your kit
- a penny
- a chair
- a tin tray or lid

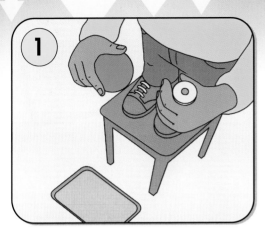

1. Place the tray on the floor in front of the chair. Stand on the chair. Hold the ball in one hand and the cotton spool and penny in the other.

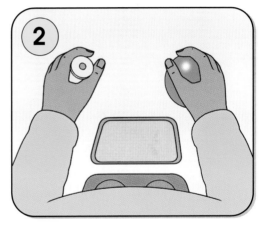

2. Hold out your arms over the tray. Make sure your hands are level (next to each other).

3. Open both hands at the same time. Listen.

Which object lands first?

2. Almost No Hands

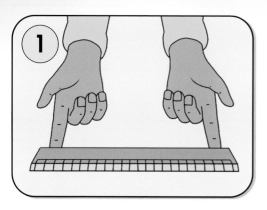

You will need:
- a ruler

1. Hold the ruler so that your hands are underneath it, palms up, one forefinger at each end of the ruler.

2. Close your eyes and take one finger away.

What happens?

Now, hold the ruler again, close your eyes and slide your fingers until they meet in the center of the ruler. Keep your hands steady and take one finger away.

What happens?

3. It's A Pushover

You will need:
- an old book that no one will mind you dropping on the floor
- a ruler

1. Place the book near the edge of a table.

2. Push it slowly towards the edge. Keep pushing.

What happens?

Glorious Gravity

1. All three objects land at the same time.

2. The first time the ruler topples and falls, the second time it stays balanced.

3. The book stays balanced until you push it too far and upset the balance, and then it falls.

They All Fall Down

In experiment 1, the objects fall because they are pulled towards the ground by the force of gravity.

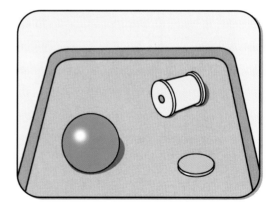

Even though the objects are different sizes and weights, they all fall together because gravity pulls all objects downward at the same speed, whatever they weigh.

Balancing Acts

Gravity makes things fall to the ground when they are dropped. All things are pulled towards the center of Earth by gravity. Every object has a point where it is held in balance by the force of gravity. This is called its 'center of gravity.'

When you slide your fingers towards the middle of the ruler, you find its center of gravity and it balances.

When you push the book towards the edge of the table, it doesn't topple until you push it past its center of gravity.

Colorific Celery

You will need:
- two tall glasses
- a leafy celery stalk
- two colors of food coloring (or water paints)
- water
- scissors

Colored Celery

1. Ask an adult to help you cut up the middle of the celery stalk with a pair of scissors. Then stand each half of the celery stalk in separate glasses.

2. Half fill the glasses with water, and add a few drops of food coloring (or water paints): one color in one glass and another color in the other glass.

3. Leave the celery for an hour. What happens to the celery? Leave the celery for another twelve hours. Now look closely at the leaves!

What happens?

Colorific Celery

Different parts of the celery have turned a different color!

Plants absorb water through their roots and suck it up their stalks along tiny tubes called vessels. When the water reaches the leaves, tiny droplets escape through little holes in the leaves.

What happens!

The little tubes, known as vessels, connect to different parts of a plant. When the colored water is sucked up by your celery, you can see which part of the plant it has been sucked up to.

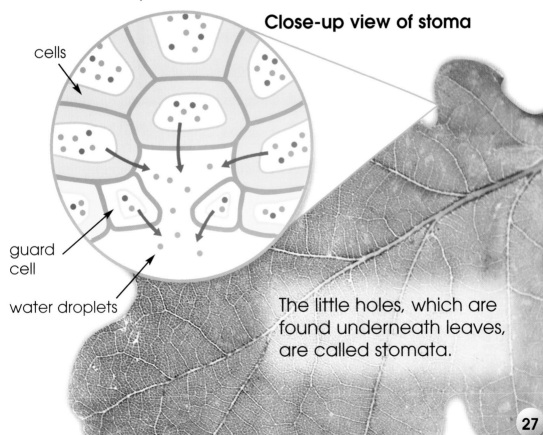

Close-up view of stoma

cells

guard cell

water droplets

The little holes, which are found underneath leaves, are called stomata.

It's Electric!

1. Jump To It!

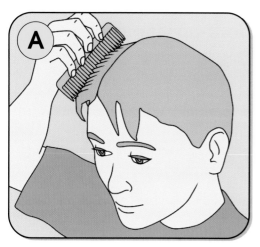

You will need:
- a plastic comb
- small pieces of paper

B. Again, pull the comb through your hair a few times before holding it near a running faucet.

What happens?

A. Pull the comb through your hair a few times. Now hold it near the pieces of paper.

What happens?

2. Balloon Tricks

You will need:
- a blown-up balloon
- thread
- sticky tape
- small, chunky cereal pieces (such as puffed wheat)

A. Rub the balloon against your hair or on a wool sweater. Press it against a wall and let go.

What happens?

It's Electric!

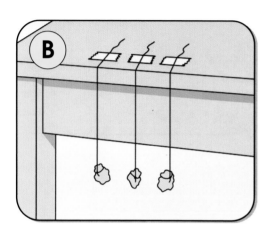

B. Tie two or three pieces of cereal to threads. Tape the threads to the edge of a flat surface so they hang down. Rub the balloon against your hair. Move it towards the dangling cereal.

What happens?

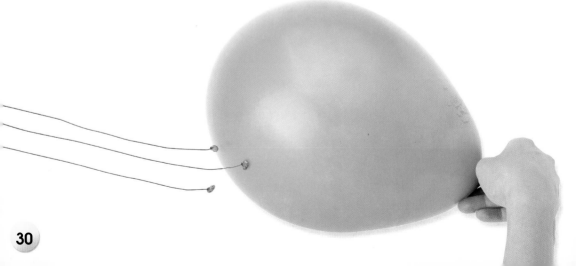

Static Electricity

If you have ever taken off your sweater and heard a crackling noise, or your hair has stuck up on end, then you have heard and seen static electricity.

Static electricity builds up when two materials, like a comb and a cloth, are rubbed together. It can pull things together or push them apart.

When a balloon sticks to the wall the two charges are sticking together.

What happens!

When you rub the comb through your hair, electricity jumps from your hair to the comb but then has nowhere to go—until you put it near some paper or water. The same thing happens when you rub the balloon.

Special Solutions

See how some liquids will magically float on top of others even when you shake them!

Warning: Ask an adult to help you before trying out these tricks!

Separate Liquids

You will need:
- goggles from your kit
- test tube from your kit
- vinegar
- vegetable oil or olive oil
- egg yolk
- funnel from your kit

1. Put on your laboratory goggles. Pour a small amount of vinegar into the test tube, using your funnel, then add a few drops of oil. Put the stopper in the test tube and shake it.

What happens?

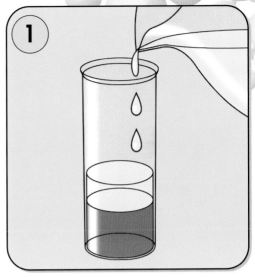

2. It takes a special ingredient to make oil and vinegar mix together. Add a small amount of egg yolk to the liquids, replace the stopper and shake.

What happens?

Special Solutions

You will need:
- goggles from your kit
- test tube from your kit
- salt
- funnel from your kit

2. Add a pinch of salt, put the stopper on the test tube and shake it. The salt will dissolve in the water. Keep adding salt, a few grains at a time.

What happens?

Sinking Salt

1. Put on your goggles to protect your eyes. Fill the test tube about three-quarters full of water, using your funnel.

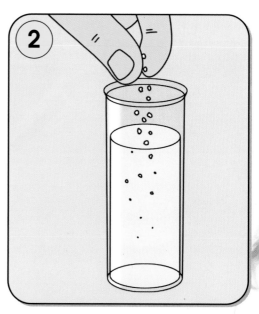

Mix It Up!

A solution is made when something solid is dissolved into liquid—just like the salt and water. Liquids can mix together too, but not all of them. Oil will sit on top of vinegar because it is much lighter.

What Happens!

When you shake up your mixture of oil and vinegar, the egg yolk acts like glue. The yolk sticks to the oil bubbles and holds them in the vinegar, stopping the liquids from separating again.

Water can only dissolve, or hold, a certain amount of salt —just like your school bags will only hold so many books! When water can't dissolve any more salt it has to stay solid and sinks to the bottom.

Fantastic Flight

1. Flying Wing

You will need:
- sheet of paper from your kit

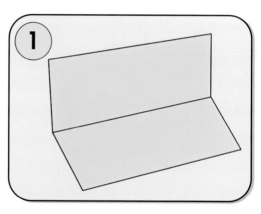

1. Fold your piece of paper lengthways, as shown in the picture, and open it out again.

2. Fold the top corners over so that they meet in the middle crease.

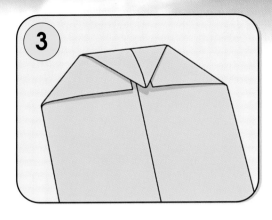

3. Fold the top point down and then the two sloping edges over to make the wings.

4. Turn the wings over and bend the two wing tips up slightly.

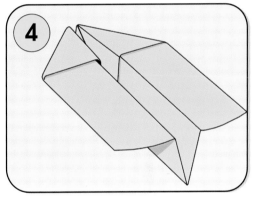

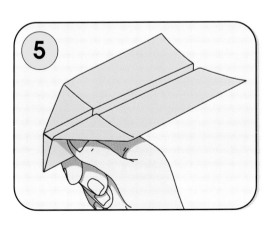

5. Hold your plane at the underneath edge and throw it forward and upward.

What happens?

Fantastic Flight

Your plane should soar and zoom across the room!

Planes stay in the sky because air pushes them up harder than gravity is pulling them down. It can only do this because of the way planes are built.

Up, Up And Away!

Gravity pulls everything downward.

Airplane wings are curved at the top. When a plane is flying, air moves over it faster than air moves under it. Slow-moving air pushes harder than fast-moving air.

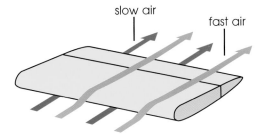

slow air

fast air

What Happens!

When you throw your paper plane, the slower-moving air underneath the wing lifts it into the air.

Balancing Boat

Sink Or Float?

Have you ever wondered why boats can float and other things can't? Try out these cool sinking and floating tricks to find out the answer!

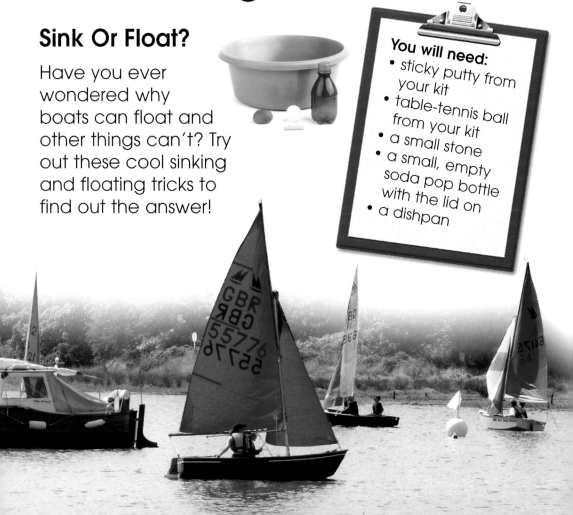

You will need:
- sticky putty from your kit
- table-tennis ball from your kit
- a small stone
- a small, empty soda pop bottle with the lid on
- a dishpan

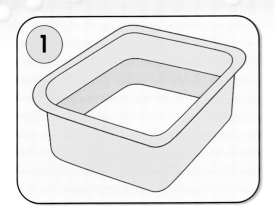

1. Ask an adult to half fill the dishpan, or your sink, with water.

2. Put the piece of sticky putty, table-tennis ball, small stone and soda pop bottle into the water.

What happens?

If you like, you can experiment with different items as well. Why not try a cotton spool, or even a feather?

Balancing Boat

3. Take the objects out of the water. Dry the sticky putty. Model it into a boat shape. Carefully put this on the water.

What happens?

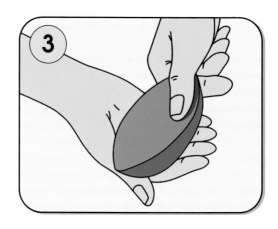

Some of the items float on top of the water and some items sink to the bottom.

Splish, Splosh, Splash!

The more water there is pushing upwards against something, the more likely it is to float. On water, something flat will spread its weight over more water than something round.

Easy Load

The lighter something is, the more likely it is to float because it will put less pressure on the water.

To make room for itself in the water, an object must push aside, or displace, an equal amount of water.

What Happens!

1. The soda pop bottle and table-tennis ball float because they both hold air, which is lighter than water.

2. The stone and solid piece of sticky putty sink because they are heavier than the water and, because they are round, only a little of them presses against the water. When you make the sticky putty flatter and build up the sides, to spread its weight, then it floats.

Surprising Spiral

You will need:
- one sheet of paper
- scissors
- thread
- a plastic adhesive hook
- sticky tape

1. Cut a spiral shape from the paper, as shown.

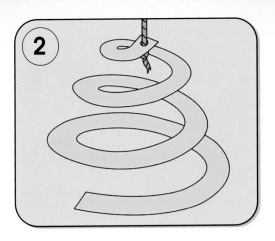

2. Make a small hole in the center and tie a length of thread to this.

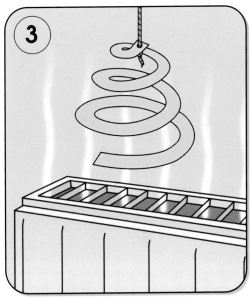

3. Tie the other end of the thread to the hook and ask an adult to hang this over a radiator, so that the spiral hangs downwards.

Or ask an adult to tape the end of the thread to the ceiling above a radiator.

What happens?

Why not draw or paint a colorful design on your paper before you cut out your spiral?

Surprising Spiral

The spiral begins to twist and turn.

What Happens!

Heat causes things to expand (get bigger). Heated air rises because it is lighter than cold air. The rising air turns the spiral.

The same thing happens in hot air balloons. The heated air inside the balloon is lighter than the cold air around it. So it rises!

Test This Out

Here's another trick to show you what the power of heat can do.

1. Put the bottle in the freezer for an hour. Take the bottle out of the freezer. Wet the top. Stick the quarter over the bottle so that it covers the mouth of the bottle.

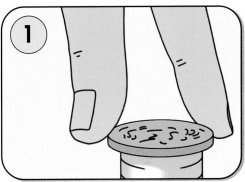

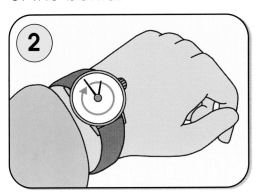

2. Put the bottle back in the freezer for an hour. Take the bottle out of the freezer.

3. Point it away from you —and anyone else!

Hold it in both hands —and wait!

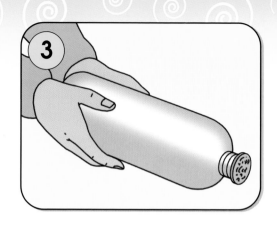

What happens?

The heat from your hands warms the air inside the bottle. The air expands—and pushes its way out of the bottle!